Langenscheidt

Spanish
at your Fingertips

Tien Tammada

Langenscheidt

Foreword

Traveling to foreign or to distant lands is a wonderful and exciting thing to do. In fact, it probably features top of the list in worldwide rankings.

However, before every journey to a foreign country, there is a hurdle to be cleared and this hurdle is called "foreign languages". For many, this hurdle seems insurmountable. As a result, they have to give up their life's dream.

What a pity!

You may be planning a week's holiday in Mexico to experience the magical countryside or considering moving to live and work in a Spanish-speaking country. You might want to flirt or just understand when someone is trying to flirt with you (after all, you don't want to miss the chance to meet the prince or princess of your dreams, do you?).

Whatever your motivation, don't wait.
Don't let this hurdle stop you from fulfilling your lifelong dreams!
Take courage to embark on this exciting journey to the Spanish language

-**now!**

Once you've made the decision, you'll find that this book provides you with the first helpful steps. You don't need to book a language course and you don't need to worry about complicated grammatical points.

Anyone who has learnt to master a foreign language knows that the essential and really crucial thing about learning a language is actually quite simple: you need to jump in at the deep end. Once you're in the water, everything flows from there.

Jump and don't think twice! You'll learn by doing, not by preparing.
The pictures, the selection of important words and useful phrases that you'll find in this book are an important first step. As soon as you come up against the first language hurdle, you can open the book at the appropriate page and find the necessary words and phrases.

If that doesn't work, try pointing to the relevant picture or sentence with your finger. People will know immediately what you mean.
It's really all very easy and convenient. That's why the book is called:

"Spanish at your Fingertips" .

Content

Useful daily conversations

Frases cotidianas, frases útiles
['frases koti'ðĭanas 'frases 'utiles]

Greeting

Saludos [sa'luðos]

¡Buenos días!	¡Buenas tardes!	¡Hola!
['bŭenos 'di:as]	['bŭenas 'tarðes]	['ola]
Good morning!	Good evening!	Hello!

¿Cómo está? / ¿Cómo estás? / ¿Qué onda?

[ˈkomo esˈta / komo esˈtas / ke ˈonda]

How are you? / What's up?

Estoy bien, gracias.

[esˈtɔĭ bĭen ˈgrasĭas]

I’m fine, thank you.

Sí.	No.
[si]	[no]
Yes.	No.

Gracias.	Muchas gracias.	De nada.	Es un placer.
['grasĭas]	['mutʃas 'grasĭas]	[de 'naða]	[es un pla'sɛr]
Thanks.	Thank you very much.	You're welcome.	With pleasure.

Me llamo... [me 'ʎamo]	My name is …
¿Cómo se llama? ['komo se 'ʎama]	What is your name? (formal)
¿Cómo te llamas? ['komo te 'ʎamas]	What is your name? (informal)
Mucho gusto. ['mutʃo 'gusto]	Nice to meet you.
Soy de Estados Unidos de América. [sɔĭ de es'taðos u'niðos de a'merika]	I'm from the United States of America.
No hablo español. [no 'aβlo espa'ɲɔl]	I don't speak Spanish.
Hablo un poco de español. ['aβlo un 'poko de espa'ɲɔl]	I speak a little Spanish.
¿Puede hablar más despacio, por favor? ['pŭeðe a'βlar mas des'pasĭo pɔr fa'βɔr]	Could you speak a little more slowly, please?
¿Cómo se llama eso en español? ['komo se 'ʎama 'eso en espa'ɲɔl]	How do you say that in Spanish?

¿Qué significa eso? [ke siɣniˈfika ˈeso]	What does that mean?
¿Qué es eso? [ke es eso]	What is that?
¡Perdone! [pɛrˈðɔne]	Sorry!
¡Disculpe! [disˈkulpe]	Excuse me!
Ningún problema. [niŋˈgun proˈβlema]	No problem.
No hay problema. [no aĭ proˈβlema]	No problem.
Señor... [seˈɲɔr]	Mr...
Señora... [seˈɲɔra]	Mrs...

Señorita... [seɲɔˈrita]	Miss...
¿Dónde está...? [ˈdɔnde esˈta]	Where is...?
Querría... [keˈrria]	I would like...
¿Cuánto cuesta? [ˈkŭanto ˈkŭesta]	How much does it cost...?
bien [bĭen]	good
muy bien [mŭi bĭen]	very good
Me gusta... [me 'gusta]	I like...
No me gusta... [no me 'gusta]	I don't like...

¡Estupendo! [estuˈpendo]	Great!
¡Qué guay! [ke gŭaĭ]	Awesome!
mal [mal]	bad
muy mal [mŭi mal]	very bad
¡Maravilloso! [maraβiˈʎoso]	Marvelous!
mucho [ˈmutʃo]	a lot
no mucho [no ˈmutʃo]	not much
un poco [un ˈpoko]	a little
Un momento, por favor. [un moˈmento pɔr faˈβɔr]	One moment, please.
Un instante, por favor. [un insˈtante pɔr faˈβɔr]	One moment, please.

¡Hasta mañana! [ˈasta maˈɲana]	See you tomorrow!
¡Adios! [aˈðĭɔs]	Bye!
¡Hasta la próxima vez! [ˈasta la ˈprɔɣsima besl]	See you next time!
¿Quién? [kĭen]	Who?
¿Qué? [ke]	What?
¿Cuándo? [ˈkŭando]	When?
¿Por qué? [pɔr ke]	Why?
¿Cómo? [ˈkomo]	How?
¿Dónde? [ˈdɔnde]	Where?
¿Cuánto? [ˈkŭanto]	How much? / How many?

At the airport

En el aeropuerto [en ɛl aero'pŭɛrto]

el aeropuerto — the airport

[ɛl aero'pŭɛrto]

¿Dónde está el control de pasaportes? — Where is the passport control?

['dɔnde es'ta ɛl kɔn'trɔl de pasa'pɔrtes]

EL AVIÓN

[ɛl a'βĭɔn]

Perdone, ¿cómo se va al centro de la ciudad?

[pɛr'ðɔne 'komo se ba al 'sentro de la sĭu'ðað]

Excuse me, how can I get to the city center?

Perdone, ¿cómo se va a la estación de tren?

[pɛr'ðɔne 'komo se ba a la esta'sĭɔn de tren]

Excuse me, where is the train station?

[saˈliða] Exit

Perdone, ¿dónde está la salida?

[pɛrˈðɔne ˈdɔnde esˈta la saˈliða]

Excuse me, where is the exit?

the airplane

¿Dónde está la parada de camión?

[ˈdɔnde esˈta la paˈraða de kaˈmjon]

Where is the bus stop?

¿Dónde está la parada de taxi?

[ˈdɔnde esˈta la paˈraða de ˈtaɣsi]

Where is the taxi stand?

¿Dónde está la oficina de información turística?
['dɔnde es'ta la ofi'sina de imfɔrma'sĭɔn turística]
Where is tourist information?

¿Cómo de lejos está el centro de la ciudad?
['komo de 'lɛxos es'ta ɛl 'sentro de la sĭu'ðað]
How far is it to the city center?

¿Conoce un hotel económico?
[ko'nosɛ un ɔ'tɛl eko'nomiko]
Do you know an inexpensive hotel?

Por favor, lléveme a esta dirección.
[pɔr fa'βɔr 'ʎeβeme a 'esta dirɛɣ'sĭɔn]
Would you please drive me to this address?

el taxi
[ɛl 'taɣsi]

taxi

¿Cuánto cuesta el viaje?
[ˈkŭanto ˈkŭesta ɛl biˈaxe]
How much does the ride cost?

¿Puedo pagar con tarjeta de crédito?
[ˈpŭeðo paˈɣar kɔn tarˈxeta de ˈkreðito]
Can I pay by credit card?

¿Podría avisarme cuándo tenga que bajarme?
[poˈðria aβiˈsarme ˈkŭando ˈteŋga ke baˈxarme]
Could you tell me when to get off please?

Muchas gracias por su ayuda.
[ˈmutʃas ˈgrasĭas pɔr su aˈjuða]
Thank you very much for your help.

el camión
[ɛl kaˈmjon]

bus

el tren

[ɛl tren]

train

el metro

[ɛl ˈmetro]

underground

el tranvía

[ɛl tramˈbia]

tram

el TAV (Tren de Alta Velocidad)

[ɛl tren de ˈalta belosiˈðað]

HST (High Speed Train)

el barco

[ɛl ˈbarko]

ship

Accommodation

El alojamiento [ɛl alɔxa'mĭento]

¿Tiene una habitación libre? ['tjene una aβita'sĭɔn 'liβre]	Is there any room available?
¿Puedo ver la habitación? ['pŭeðo bɛr la aβita'sĭɔn]	May I see the room, please?
¿Cuánto cuesta? ['kŭanto 'kŭesta]	How much is it?
¿Está incluido el desayuno? [es'ta iŋklu'ido ɛl desa'juno]	Is breakfast included?
He reservado una habitación a nombre de… [e rrɛsɛr'βaðo 'una aβita'sĭɔn a 'nɔmbre de]	I have booked a room in the name of...
Aquí tiene mi pasaporte. [a'ki 'tĭene mi pasa'pɔrte]	Here is my passport.

¿Hay wifi en el hotel?

[aĭ ˈŭifi en ɛl ɔˈtɛl]

Do you have Wi-Fi?

¿Hay una caja fuerte para los efectos personales?

[aĭ ˈuna ˈkaxa ˈfŭɛrte ˈpara lɔs eˈfɛktos pɛrsoˈnales]

Do you have a safe?

¿Cuándo tengo que dejar la habitación?

[ˈkŭando ˈteŋgo ke dɛˈxar la aβitaˈsĭɔn]

When do I have to check out?

¿La recepción está abierta las 24 horas?

[la rresepˈsĭɔn esˈta aˈβĭerta las beĭnti ˈkŭatro ˈoras]

Is reception open all the time?

Querría una habitación para...

[ke'rria 'una aβita'sĭɔn 'para]

I would like a room for...

una persona.

['una pɛr'sona]

one (person).

dos personas.

[dɔs pɛr'sonas]

two (people).

una familia.
['una fa'milĭa]

a family.

la lámpara de techo
[la ˈlampara de ˈtetʃo]
ceiling lamp
la estantería
[la estanteˈria]
bookshelf
la lámpara
[la ˈlampara]
lamp
la ventana
[la benˈtana]
window
el interruptor
[ɛl intɛrrupˈtɔr]
light switch
el despertador
[ɛl despɛrtaˈðɔr]
alarm clock
la almohada
[la almoˈaða]
pillow
la silla
[la ˈsiʎa]
chair
el escritorio
[ɛl eskriˈtorĭo]
desk
el enchufe
[ɛl enˈtʃufe]
electric socket

In the bedroom

En el dormitorio [en ɛl dɔrmiˈtorĭo]

In the bathroom

En el baño [en ɛl 'baɲo]

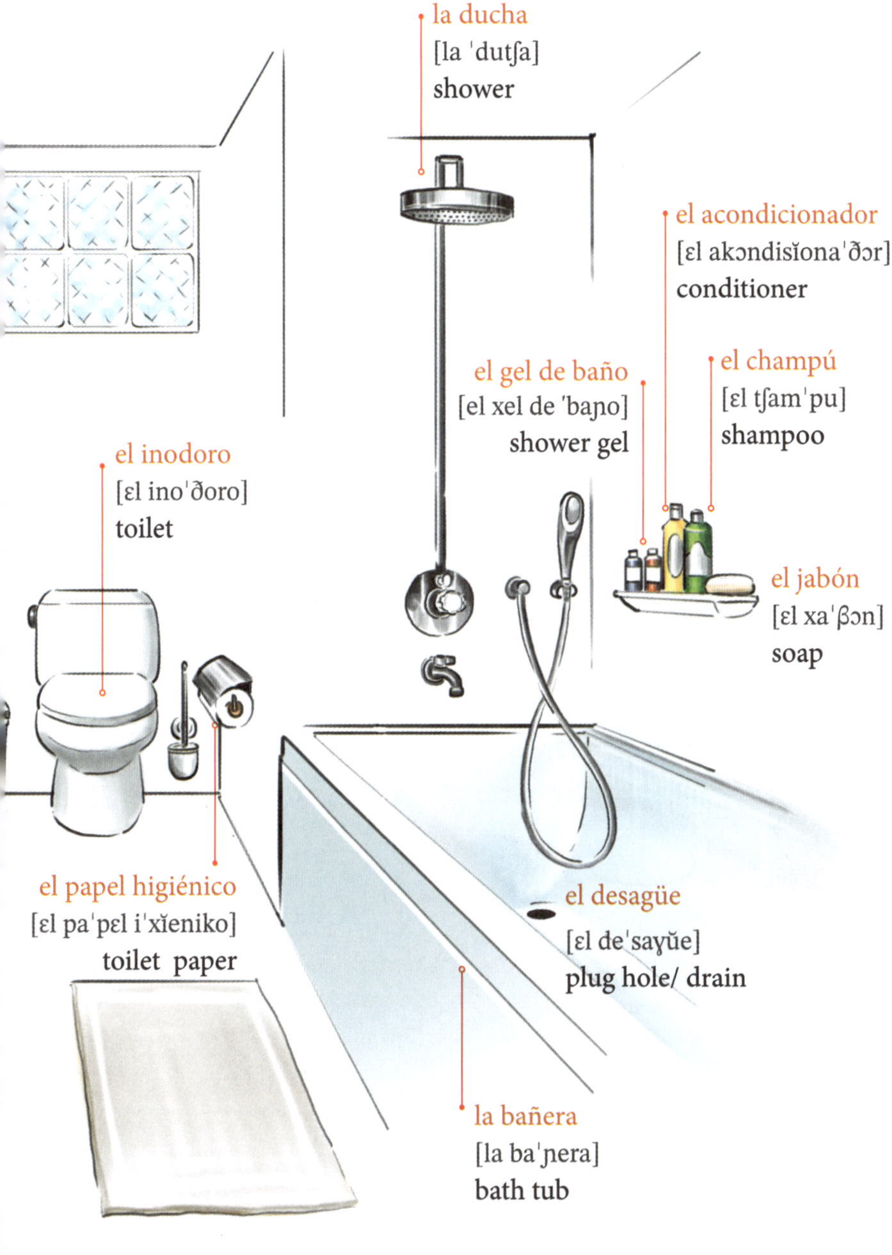
la ducha
[la ˈdutʃa]
shower
el acondicionador
[ɛl akɔndisĭonaˈðɔr]
conditioner
el gel de baño
[el xel de ˈbaɲo]
shower gel
el champú
[ɛl tʃamˈpu]
shampoo
el inodoro
[ɛl inoˈðoro]
toilet
el jabón
[ɛl xaˈβɔn]
soap
el papel higiénico
[ɛl paˈpɛl iˈxĭeniko]
toilet paper
el desagüe
[ɛl deˈsaɣŭe]
plug hole/ drain
la bañera
[la baˈɲera]
bath tub

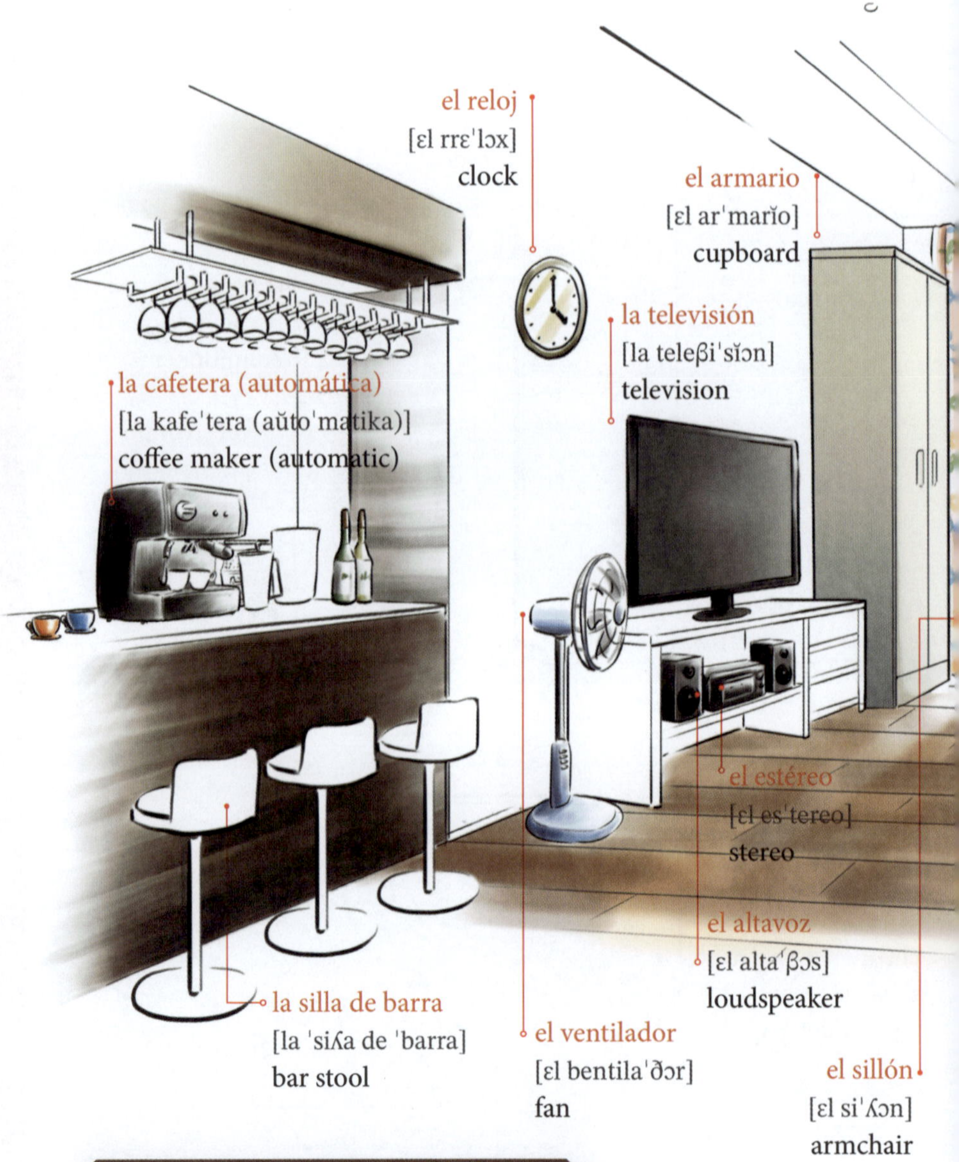

In the living room

En el salón [en ɛl saˈlɔn]

el piano
[ɛl ˈpĭano]
piano
el cuadro
[ɛl ˈkŭaðro]
picture
el violín
[ɛl bĭoˈlin]
violin
el teléfono
[ɛl teˈlefono]
telephone
el sofá
[ɛl soˈfa]
sofa
el florero
[ɛl floˈrero]
vase
el control remoto
[ɛl konˈtrol remoto]
remote control
la flor
[la flɔr]
flowers

la sartén
[la sar'ten]
frying pan
la taza
[la 'tasa]
cup
la botella
[la bo'teʎa]
bottle
la copa de vino
[la 'kopa de 'bino]
wine glass
el plato
[ɛl 'plato]
plate
la cuchara
[la ku'tʃara]
spoon
el tenedor
[ɛl tene'ðɔr]
fork
la tabla
[la 'taβla]
chopping board
el grifo
[ɛl 'grifo]
faucet
el microondas
[ɛl micro'ondas]
microwave

In the kitchen

En la cocina [en la koˈsina]

Excursions (In the city and in the countryside)

Excursiones (en la ciudad y fuera) [eskur'sĭɔnes (en la sĭu'ðað i 'fŭera)]

¿Qué lugares interesantes hay por aquí?

[ke lu'ɣares intere'santes ai por a'ki]

Are there any tourist attractions in this area?

¿Dondé puedo probar la comida local?

['dɔnde 'pŭeðo pro'βar la ko'miða lo'kal]

Where can I taste the traditional local food?

Excursions by train

Excursiones en tren
[eskur'sĭɔnes en tren]

¿Dónde está la estación de tren? | Where is the train station?
['dɔnde es'ta la esta'sĭɔn de tren]

¿Dónde está la taquilla? | Where is the ticket office?
['dɔnde es'ta la ta'kiʎa]

¿Cuánto cuesta el billete? | How much does the ticket cost?
['kŭanto 'kŭesta ɛl bi'ʎete]

Por favor, un billete de primera clase. | One first-class ticket, please.
[pɔr fa'βɔr un bi'ʎete de pri'mera 'klase]

Por favor, un billete de segunda clase. | One second-class ticket, please.
[pɔr fa'βɔr un 'bi'ʎete de se'ɣunda 'klase]

Un billete de ida, por favor. | A one-way ticket, please.
[un bi'ʎete de 'iða pɔr fa'βɔr]

Un billete de ida y vuelta, por favor. | A return ticket, please.
[un bi'ʎete de 'iða i 'bŭɛlta pɔr fa'βɔr]

Querría reservar un asiento.
[keˈrria rrɛsɛrˈβar un aˈsĭento]

I would like to reserve a seat, please.

¿A qué hora sale el tren?
[a ke ˈora ˈsale ɛl tren]

What time does the train leave?

¿Cuántos transbordos tengo que hacer?
[ˈkŭantos transˈβorðos ˈteŋgo ke aˈsɛr]

How many times do I have to change trains?

¿Cómo se llama la próxima estación?
[ˈkomo se ˈʎama la ˈprɔɣsima estaˈsĭɔn]

What is the next station called?

¿Podría avisarme cuándo tenga que bajarme?
[poˈðria aβiˈsarme ˈkŭando ˈteŋga ke baˈxarme]

Would you please tell me when I have to get off?

At the train station

En la estación de tren [en la esta'sĭɔn de tren]

la estación
[la esta'sĭɔn]
station

la estación central
[la esta'sĭɔn sen'tral]
central station

la taquilla
[la ta'kiʎa]
ticket office

el billete
[ɛl bi'ʎete]
ticket

los horarios
[los o'rarĭos]
timetable

la llegada
[la ʎe'ɣaða]
arrival

la salida
[la sa'liða]
departure

el tren
[ɛl tren]
train

el andén
[ɛl an'den]
platform

el coche cama
[ɛl 'kotʃe 'kama]
sleeping carriage

el tren rápido
[ɛl tren 'rrapiðo]
express train

un billete de primera clase
[un biˈʎete de priˈmera ˈklase]
a first-class ticket

un billete de segunda clase
[un ˈbiˈʎete de seˈɣunda ˈklase]
a second-class ticket

una reserva de asiento
[una rrɛˈsɛrβa de aˈsĭento]
seat reservation

ida y vuelta
[ˈiðа i ˈbŭɛlta]
return

solo ida
[ˈsolo ˈiða]
one-way

el suplemento
[ɛl supleˈmento]
surcharge

subir al tren
[suˈβir al tren]
board

bajar del tren
[baˈxar dɛl tren]
get off

hacer transbordo(s)
[aˈsɛr transˈβorðo(s)]
change trains

¿A qué hora va a salir el tren / el camión / el metro /el tranvía?

[a ke 'ora va a sa'lir ɛl tren / ɛl ka'mjon /

ɛl 'metro / ɛl tram'bia]

What time does the train / the bus
the underground / the tram leave?

Disculpe, ¿puede ayudarme a comprar el billete en la máquina expendedora?

[dis'kulpe 'pŭeðe aju'ðarme a kɔm'prar ɛl bi'ʎete en la 'makina espende'ðora]

Excuse me, can you help me to buy a ticket from the machine?

Quiero ir a...

['kĭero ir a]

I want to go to...

Excursions by bus and tram

Excursiones en camión y en tranvía
[eskur'sĭɔnes en ka'mjon i en tram'bia]

el camión — bus
[ɛl ka'mjon]

la parada de camión — bus stop
[la pa'raða de ka'mjon]

el tranvía — tram
[ɛl tram'bia]

¿Dónde está la parada de tranvía?
['dɔnde es'ta la pa'raða de tram'bia]
Where is the tram stop?

la parada de tranvía — tram stop
[la pa'raða de tram'bia]

el billete — ticket
[ɛl bi'ʎete]

el controlador, la controladora — ticket inspector
[ɛl/la kɔntrola'ðɔr(a)]

la multa — fine/penalty
[la 'multa]

¿Dónde está...?

[ˈdɔnde esˈta]

Where is…?

¿Dónde está la parada de camión?

[ˈdɔnde esˈta la paˈraða de kaˈmjon]

Where is the bus stop?

el semáforo
[ɛl seˈmaforo]
traffic lights

la motocicleta
[la motosiˈkleta]
motorcycle

la bicicleta
[la bisiˈkleta]
bicycle

el carro
[ɛl ˈkaro]
car

Traveling on your own by car, motocycle, bicycle and on foot

Viajar por su cuenta en coche, motocicleta, bicicleta y a pie
[bĭa'xar pɔr su 'kŭenta en 'kotʃe, motosi'kleta, bisi'kleta i a pĭe]

la calle [la 'kaʎe]	street
la intersección [la intɛrsɛɣ'sĭɔn]	intersection
el paso de cebra [ɛl 'paso de 'seβra]	pedestrian crossing
todo recto ['toðo 'rrɛkto]	go straight on
a la derecha [a la de'retʃa]	to the right
a la izquierda [a la is'kĭɛrða]	to the left
¿Dónde hay una gasolinera? ['dɔnde aĭ 'una gasoli'nera]	Where is a petrol station?
acá / allá [a'ka / a'ʎa]	here / there
cerca / lejos ['sɛrka / 'lɛxos]	near / far

Art and leisure time activities

Arte y actividades de tiempo libre ['arte i aktiβi'ðaðes de 'tjempo 'liβre]

el teatro

[ɛl te'atro]

the theater

---

la ópera

[la 'opera]

the opera house

---

el cine

[ɛl 'sine]

the cinema

---

la galería de arte

[la gale'ria de 'arte]

the art gallery

---

el museo

[ɛl mu'seo]

the museum

la alberca cubierta

[la al'βɛrka ku'βĭɛrta]

the indoor swimming pool

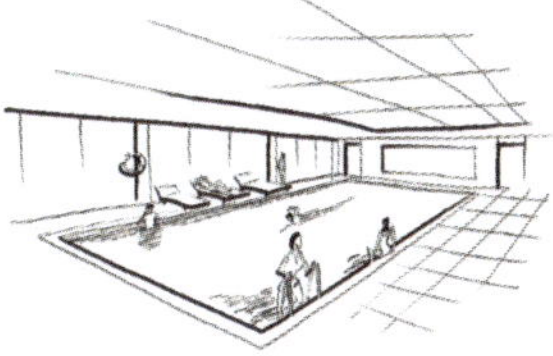

---

la alberca exterior

[la al'βɛrka este'rĭɔr]

the outdoor swimming pool

---

la sauna

[la 'saŭna]

the sauna

---

el parque municipal

[ɛl 'parke munisi'pal]

the city park

---

el gimnasio

[ɛl xim'nasĭo]

the gym

Tourist attractions

Lugares de interés turístico [lu'ɣares de inte'res tu'ristiko]

Uxmal

[uks'mal]

Pirámides de Teotihuacán

[pi'ramiðes de teotiŭa'kan]

Oaxaca

[o'waka]

Ciudad de México

[sĭu'ðað de 'mexiko]

Huasteca Potosina San Luis Potosi

[ŭasˈteka potoˈsina san ˈlŭis poˈtesi]

Cenotes de Yucatán Península

[seˈnotes de jukaˈtan peˈninsula]

Tulum

[taˈlum]

Costa Oaxaquena
Puerto Escondido

[ˈkosta owaˈkena ˈpwerto eskonˈdiðo]

Chichén Itzá

[ʧi'ʧen it'sa]

Guadalajara

['gwadala'xara]

Guanajuato

[guanaˈxŭanto]

Iglesia de santa prisca en Taxco

[iˈɣlesja de santa ˈpriska en ˈtaksko]

Cancún

[kaŋˈkun]

Barrancas del cobre

[baˈraŋkas dɛl ˈkoβɾe]

Isla mujeres

[ˈisla muˈxɛres]

Puerto Escondido, Oaxaca

[ˈpwerto eskonˈdiðo oˈwaka]

At the bakery

En la Panadería [en la panaðe'ria]

la telera

[la te'lera]

telera roll

ojos-de-buey

['oxos de bwej]

ojos de buey (sweet bread)

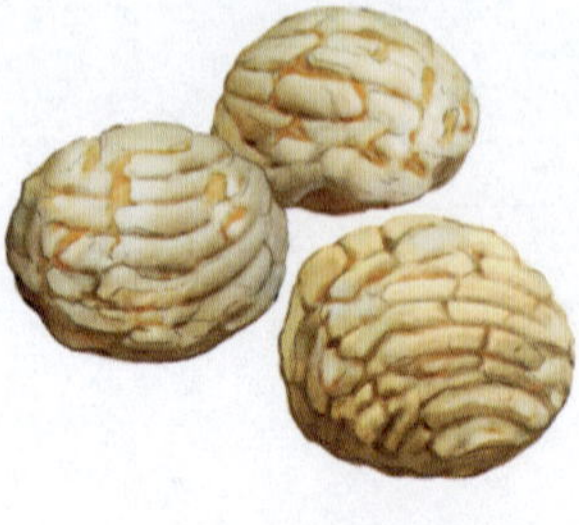

la concha

[la 'kontʃa]

concha

orejas

[o'rexas]

orejas (sweet bread)

los panecillos

[los paneˈsiʎos]

bread rolls

el pan multicereal

[ɛl pan multisereˈal]

cereal bread

el pan de semitas

[ɛl pan de semitas]

Mexican-Style roll

el cordero
[ɛl kɔrˈðero]
lamb

el pato
[ɛl ˈpato]
duck

el conejo
[ɛl koˈnɛxo]
rabbit

el pollo
[ɛl ˈpoʎo]
chicken

la ternera
[la terˈnera]
veal

At the butchers

En la carnicería [en la karniseˈria]

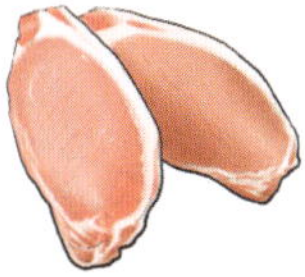

el cerdo
[ɛl ˈsɛrðo]
pork

el jamón
[ɛl xaˈmon]
ham

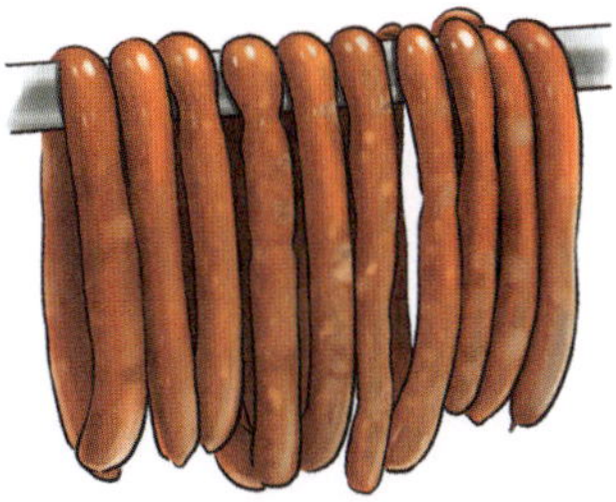

la longaniza
[la lɔŋgaˈnisa]
sausage

el chorizo
[ɛl tʃoˈriso]
sausage

At the fishmonger

En la pescadería [en la peskaðeˈria]

la trucha
[la ˈtrutʃa]
trout

el pescado
[ɛl pesˈkaðo]
fish

la ostra
[la ˈɔstra]
oyster

el cangrejo
[ɛl kaŋˈgrɛxo]
crab

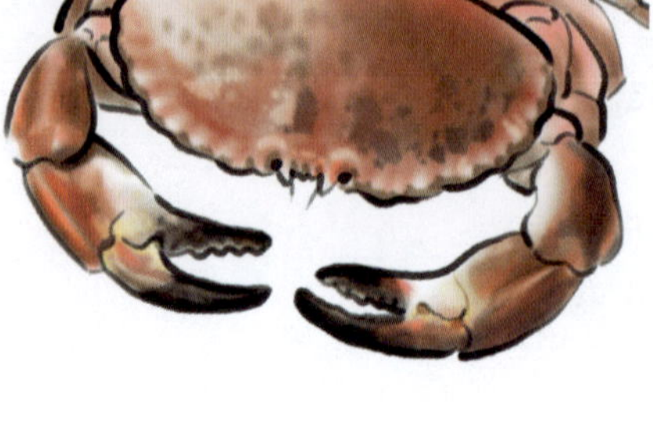

el camarón
[ɛl kamaˈron]
shrimp

el atún
[ɛl aˈtun]
tuna

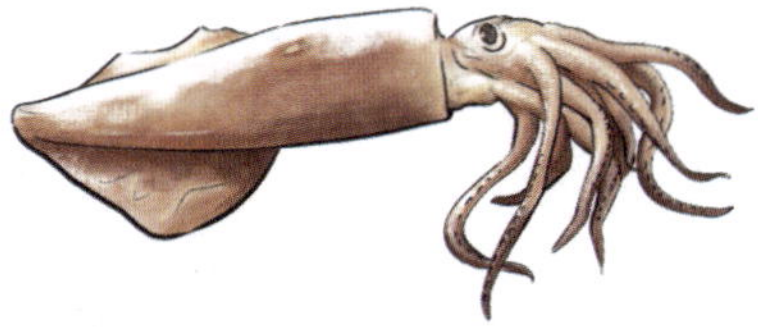

el calamar
[ɛl kalaˈmar]
squid

el salmón
[ɛl salˈmɔn]
salmon

el mejillón
[ɛl mɛxiˈʎɔn]
mussel

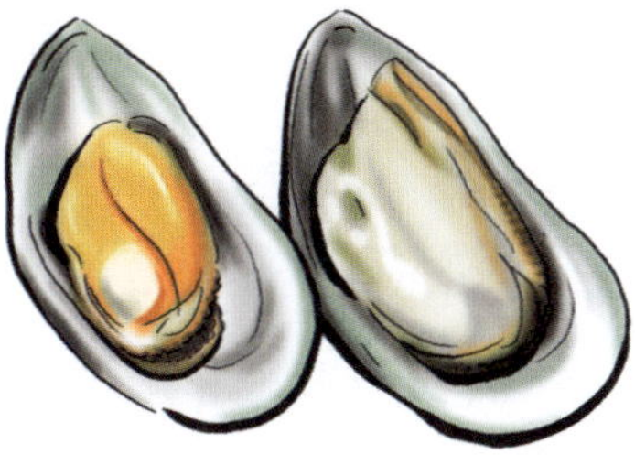

el bacalao
[ɛl bakaˈlao]
cod

1
2
3
4
5
6
7
8
9

In the vegetable shop

En la verdulería [en la bɛrðule'ria]

1. la berenjena
[la bereŋ'xena] **aubergine**

2. el pepino
[ɛl pe'pino] **cucumber**

3. el brócoli
[ɛl 'brokoli] **broccoli**

4. la alcachofa
[la alka'tʃofa] **artichoke**

5. la col china
[la kɔl 'tʃɪna] **chinese cabbage**

6. el chícharo
[ɛl 'tʃɪtʃaro] **pea**

7. la coliflor
[la koli'flɔr] **cauliflower**

8. la zanahoria
[la sana'orĭa] **carrot**

9. la albahaca
[la alβa'aka] **basil**

1. el jengibre

[ɛl xeŋˈxiβre] ginger

2. la lechuga

[la leˈtʃuɣa] lettuce

3. la calabaza

[la kalaˈβasa] pumpkin

4. la almendra

[la alˈmendra] almond

5. el cacahuate

[ɛl kakaˈŭate] peanut

6. la avellana

[la aβeˈʎana] hazelnut

7. el ajo

[ɛl ˈaxo] garlic

8. la seta

[la ˈseta] mushroom

9. la papa

[la ˈpapa] potato

10. el elote / maíz

[ɛl eˈlote/ maˈis] corn

11. la nuez

[la ˈnŭes] walnut

1
2
3
4
7
5
6
8
9
10
11

1
2
3
4
5
6
7
8
9
10

1. la remolacha

[la rrɛmoˈlatʃa] beetroot

2. el pimiento

[ɛl piˈmjento] sweet pepper

3. la cebolla

[la seˈβoʎa] onion

4. el repollo

[ɛl rrɛˈpoʎo] white cabbage

5. el repollo morado

[ɛl rrɛˈpoʎo moˈraðo] red cabbage

6. el espárrago

[ɛl esˈparraɣo] asparagus

7. el tomate

[ɛl toˈmate] tomato

8. el calabacín

[ɛl kalaβaˈsin] courgette

9. el apio

[ɛl ˈapĭo] celery

10. la espinaca

[la espiˈnaka] spinach

la manzana
[la man'sana]
apple

la manzana verde
[la man'sana 'bɛrðe]
green apple

la pera
['la 'pera]
pear

la cereza
[la se'resa]
cherry

la ciruela
[la si'rŭela]
plum

el coco
[ɛl 'koko]
coconut

la fresa
[la 'fresa]
strawberry

la piña
[la 'piɲa]
pineapple

la granada
[la graˈnaða]
pomegranate

la zarzamora
[la sarsaˈmora]
blackberry

la frambuesa
[la framˈbŭesa]
raspberry

In the fruit shop

En la frutería [en la fruteˈria]

el arándano
[ɛl aˈrandano]
blueberry

la grosella negra
[la groˈseʎa ˈneɣra]
blackcurrant

la grosella
[la groˈseʎa]
redcurrant

el limón (verde)
[ɛl liˈmɔn (ˈbɛrðe)]
lime

el limón (amarillo)
[ɛl liˈmɔn (amaˈriʎo)]
lemon

el aguacate
[ɛl aɣŭaˈkate]
avocado

el durazno
[ɛl duˈrasno]
peach

la papaya
[la paˈpaja]
papaya

el plátano
[ɛl ˈplatano]
banana

el mango
[ɛl ˈmaŋgo]
mango

la naranja
[la na'raŋxa]
orange

la mandarina
[la manda'rina]
tangerine

la sandía
[la san'dia]
watermelon

la uva
[la 'uβa]
grape

el melón
[ɛl me'lɔn]
melon

el kiwi
[ɛl 'kiβi]
kiwi

Beverages

Bebidas [be'βiðas]

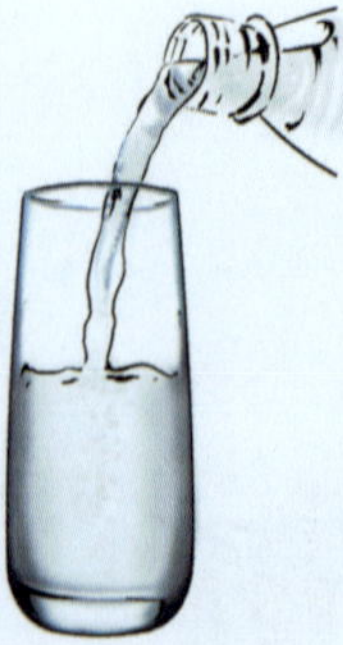

el agua
[ɛl 'aɣŭa]
still water

el agua con gas
[ɛl 'aɣŭa kon gas]
sparkling water

el agua mineral
[ɛl 'aɣŭa mineral]
mineral water

la michelada
[la mitʃe'laða]
mixed beer,
tomato juice and lime juice

la cerveza margarita
[la sɛr'βesa marɣa'rita]
beer margarita

el paloma cóctel
[ɛl pa'loma 'koktel]
mixed tequila,
lime juice and grapefruit soda

el jugo de melocotón
[ɛl 'xuɣo de meloko'tɔn]
peach juice

el jugo de piña
[ɛl 'xuɣo de 'piɲa]
pineapple juice

el jugo de manzana
[ɛl 'xuɣo de man'sana]
apple juice

el sjugo de zanahoria
[ɛl 'xuɣo de sana'oria]
carrot juice

el jugo de naranja
[ɛl 'xuɣo de na'raŋxa]
orange juice

el jugo de uva
[ɛl 'xuɣo de 'uβa]
grape juice

el jugo de tomate
[ɛl 'xuɣo de to'mate]
tomato juice

At the bar

En el bar [en ɛl bar]

la cerveza
[la sɛrˈβesa]
beer

el tequila
[ɛl teˈkila]
tequila

el vino tinto
[ɛl ˈbino ˈtinto]
red wine

el vino blanco
[ɛl ˈbino ˈblaŋko]
white wine

el vino rosado
[ɛl ˈbino rrɔˈsaðo]
rosé wine

el whisky
[ɛl ˈgŭiski]
whiskey

el coñac
[ɛl kɔˈɲak]
cognac

La vida
es demasiado
corta
para beber
vino
malo.

[la ˈbiða es demaˈsĭaðo ˈkɔrta ˈpara beˈβɛr ˈbino ˈmalo]

Life is too short to drink bad wine.

Johann Wolfgang von Goethe

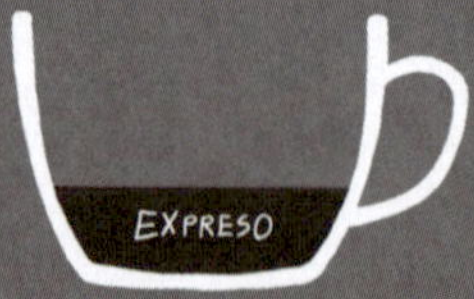

el café solo
[ɛl ka'fe 'solo]

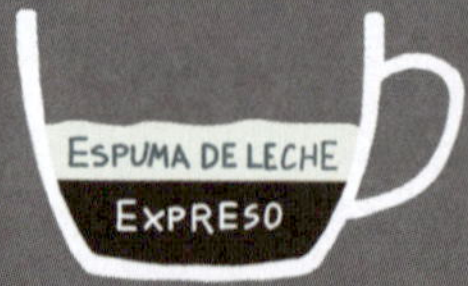

el café cortado
[ɛl ka'fe kɔr'taðo]

el café con helado
[ɛl ka'fe kɔn e'laðo]

el café con hielo
[ɛl ka'fe kɔn 'jelo]

At the coffee shop

En la cafetería [en la kafete'ria]

el café solo
coffee with a very strong taste

el café cortado
double espresso with a little milk foam

el café solo
coffee with ice cream

el café solo
coffee with ice

el café con leche
[ɛl ka'fe kɔn 'letʃe]

el cappuccino
[ɛl kapu'tʃiːno]

el café moka
[ɛl ka'fe 'moka]

el chocolate caliente
[ɛl tʃoko'late ka'lĭente]

la leche caliente
[la 'letʃe ka'lĭente]

el café con leche
milk coffee

el cappuccino
milk coffee with little milk froth

el café moka
espresso with chocolate sauce and milk foam

el chocolate caliente hot chocolat

la leche caliente hot milk

1

2

3

Tea

té [te]

4

5

6

1. el té negro
[ɛl te ˈneɣro]
black tea

2. el té blanco
[ɛl te ˈblaŋko]
white tea

3. el té verde
[ɛl te ˈbɛrðe]
green tea

4. el té afrutado
[ɛl te afruˈtaðo]
fruit tea

5. el té con limón
[ɛl te kon liˈmon]
tea with lemon

6. el té de hierbas
[ɛl te de ˈjɛrβas]
herbal tea

Disculpe, querría pedir la comida.

[dis'kulpe ke'rria pe'ðir la ko'miða]

Excuse me, I would like to order, please.

¿Cuál es la especialidad de la región?

[kŭal es la espesĭali'ðað de la rrɛ'xĭɔn]

What are the specialties of this region?

In the restaurant

En el restaurante [en ɛl rrestaŭˈrante]

el restaurante [ɛl rrestaŭˈrante] restaurant

el menú [ɛl meˈnu] menu

el entrante [ɛl enˈtrante] starter

el plato principal [ɛl ˈplato prinsiˈpal] main course

el postre [ɛl ˈpɔstre] dessert

¿Tiene mesa para dos?
[ˈtĭene ˈmesa ˈpara dɔs]

Do you have a table for two?

¿Tienen menú del día?
[ˈtĭenen meˈnu dɛl ˈdia]

What is today's special?

¿Qué me recomienda?
[ke me rrɛkomĭenˈda]

What would you recommend?

Querría...

[keˈrria]

I would like…

1. el tenedor para aperitivo
   [ɛl tene'ðɔr 'para aperi'tiβo] salad fork
2. el tenedor de plato principal
   [ɛl tene'ðɔr de 'plato prinsi'pal] dinner fork
3. el cuchillo de plato principal
   [ɛl ku'tʃiʎo de 'plato prinsi'pal] dinner knife
4. el cuchillo para aperitivo
   [ɛl ku'tʃiʎo 'para aperi'tiβo] salad knife
5. la cuchara para sopa
   [la ku'tʃara 'para 'sopa] soup spoon
6. el cuchillo de pan
   [ɛl ku'tʃiʎo de pan] butter knife
7. el tenedor para tarta
   [ɛl tene'ðɔr 'para 'tarta] dessert fork
8. la cuchara para café
   [la ku'tʃara 'para ka'fe] coffee spoon
9. el plato para pan
   [ɛl 'plato 'para pan] bread plate
10. el plato llano
    [ɛl 'plato 'ʎano] main plate
11. la copa de agua
    [la 'kopa de 'aɣŭa] water glass
12. la copa de vino tinto
    [la 'kopa de 'bino 'tinto] red wine glass
13. la copa de vino blanco
    [la 'kopa de 'bino 'blaŋko] white wine glass

Formal table setting

Protocolo en la mesa [proto'kolo en la 'mesa]

la pimienta
[la piˈmĭenta]
pepper

la sal
[la sal]
salt

Seasonings

Las especias [las esˈpesĭas]

la cayena en polvo
[la kaˈjena en ˈpolβo]
chili powder

la salsa de pesto
[la ˈsalsa de ˈpesto]
pesto

el curry
[ɛl ˈkurri]
curry powder

la mostaza
[la mɔsˈtasa]
mustard

el kétchup
[ɛl ˈkeðʧup]
ketchup

la mayonesa
[la majoˈnesa]
mayonnaise

el azúcar
[ɛl aˈsukar]
sugar

el edulcorante
[ɛl eðulkoˈrante]
sweetener

el pimentón
[ɛl pimenˈtɔn]
paprika powder

el queso parmesano
[ɛl ˈkeso parmeˈsano]
parmesan

la salsa de soja
[la ˈsalsa de ˈsɔxa]
soy sauce

la comida [la ko'miða]	meal
el desayuno [ɛl desa'juno]	breakfast
el almuerzo [ɛl almu'ɛrso]	lunch
la cena [la 'sena]	dinner

¡Buen provecho!
[bŭen pro'βetʃo]

Enjoy your meal!

La cuenta, por favor.

[la ˈkŭenta pɔr faˈβɔr]

May I have the bill, please?

¡Muy buena, la comida! [mŭi ˈbŭena la koˈmiða]	The food was very good!
¡Delicioso! [deliˈsĭoso]	Delicious!
Aquí tiene. [aˈki ˈtĭene]	Keep the change.
la propina [la proˈpina]	tip

la mermelada
[la mɛrme'laða]
jam

la miel
[la mĭɛl]
honey

la mantequilla de cacahuate
[la mante'kiʎa de kaka'ŭate]
peanut butter

la mantequilla
[la mante'kiʎa]
butter

el queso
[ɛl 'keso]
cheese

la tostada
[la tɔs'taða]
toast

el chocolate con churros
[ɛl tʃoko'late kon 'tʃurros]
chocolate with churros

el huevo cocido
[ɛl 'ŭeβo ko'siðo]
soft-boiled egg

el chocolate caliente con especias
[ɛl tʃoko'late ka'lĭente kon es'pesĭas]
Mexican spiced hot chocolate

Breakfast

El desayuno [ɛl desaˈjuno]

el muesli
[ɛl ˈmŭesli]
cereal

la macedonia
[la maseˈðonĭa]
fruit salad

el yogur
[ɛl joˈɣur]
yogurt

el huevo frito
[ɛl ˈŭeβo ˈfrito]
fried egg

las tortitas
[las tɔrˈtitas]
pancakes

el pan con tomate
[ɛl pan kɔn toˈmate]
bread with tomato

los huevos revueltos
[lɔs ˈŭeβos rrɛˈβŭɛltos]
scrambled eggs

Typical Mexican Food

Comida típica mexicana [koˈmiða ˈtipika mexiˈkana]

Aguachile
[ˈaɣŭaˈtʃɪle]
Mexican style shrimp ceviche

Huevos rancheros
[ˈŭeβos ranˈˈtʃerros]
fried eggs served on
a lightly fried corn tortillas

Chiles en nogada
[tʃiles en noɣaða]
chiles in walnut sauce

Machaca
[matʃaka]
ground dried meat
fried with egg and onion

Burritos
[bu'rritos]
flour tortilla wrapped around a filling

Quesadilla
[kesa'ðiʎa]
wheat tortilla filled with cheese, meat and vegetables

Tacos
['takos]
crispy tortilla topped with a filling

Tamales
[ta'males]
minced and seasoned meat wrapped in corn husks

Menudo
[me'nuðo]
spicy soup made with tripe.

Sopa Azteca
['sopa as'teka]
tortilla soup

Dessert

Los dulces [lɔs ˈdulses]

1. Carlota de Limón [karˈlota de liˈmɔn]

•••

2. Churros [ˈtʃurros]

•••

3. Cocadas [koˈkaðas]

•••

4. Conchas (Pan Dulce) [ˈkɔntʃas (pan ˈdulses)]

•••

5. Flan [flan]

•••

6. Fresas Con Crema [ˈfresas kɔn ˈkrema]

•••

7. Polvorones [polβoɾones]

•••

8. Pastel de Elote [pasˈtel de eˈlote]

•••

9. Sopaipillas [sopaiˈpiʎas]

•••

10. Bionicos [biˈonkos]

•••

11. Pastel de tres leches [pasˈtel de tres ˈletʃes]

•••

12. Arroz Con Leche [aˈros kon ˈletʃe]

1

2

3

4

5

6

7

8

9

10

11

12

Places to shop

Tiendas y supermercados ['tĭendas i supɛrmɛr'kaðos]

el centro comercial

[ɛl ˈsentro komɛrˈsĭal] shopping center

la tienda

[la ˈtĭenda] shop

el mercado

[ɛl mɛrˈkaðo] market

el supermercado

[ɛl supɛrmɛrˈkaðo] supermarket

el quiosco

[ɛl ˈkĭɔsko] kiosk

Everything your heart desires

Todo lo que el corazón desea [ˈtoðo lo ke ɛl koraˈsɔn deˈsea]

la tienda de cosméticos
[la ˈtĭenda de kɔzˈmetikos]
cosmetic shop

---

la peluquería
[la pelukeˈria]
hair salon

---

la joyería
[la xojeˈria]
jewellery shop

---

la floristería
[la floristeˈria]
flower shop

la tienda de moda
[la 'tĭenda de 'moða]
fashion boutique

la zapatería
[la sapate'ria]
shoe shop

la tienda de souvenirs
[la 'tĭenda de sube'nirs]
souvenir shopp

la tienda de antigüedades
[la 'tĭenda de antiɣŭe'ðaðes]
antique shop

Quiero… [ˈkĭero]	I would like…
una camisa. [ˈuna kaˈmisa]	a shirt.
un pantalón. [un pantaˈlɔn]	a pair of trousers.
un par de zapatos. [un par de saˈpatos]	a pair of shoes.
unas medias. [ˈunas ˈmeðĭas]	a pair of socks.
dos blusas. [dɔs ˈblusas]	two blouses.
tres chamarra. [tres tʃaˈmara]	three jackets.
cuatro faldas. [ˈkŭatro ˈfaldas]	four skirts.
un abrigo. [un aˈβriɣo]	five coats.

¿Cuánto cuesta esto? ['kŭanto 'kŭesta 'esto]	How much does it cost?
Cuesta ... pesos. ['kŭesta ... 'pesos]	It costs ... pesos.
Es muy caro. [es mŭi 'karo]	That is very expensive.
Es muy barato. [es mŭi ba'rato]	That is very cheap.
Gracias, es suficiente. ['grasĭas es sufi'sĭente]	That's fine, thanks.
Es económico. [es eko'nomiko]	The price is reasonable.
Es demasiado corto / largo. [es dema'sĭaðo 'kɔrto(a) / 'larɣo(a)]	It's too short / too long.
Es demasiado estrecho / ancho. [es dema'sĭaðo es'tretʃo / 'antʃo]	It's too tight / too loose.

¿Puedo probármelo?

[ˈpŭeðo proˈβarmelo]

May I try it on?

¿Dónde está el probador?

[ˈdɔnde esˈta ɛl proβaˈðɔr]

Where is the fitting room?

Rebajado

[rrεβaxa'ðo]

discounted

precio rebajado

['presĭo rrεβa'xado] reduced price

liquidación

[likiða'sĭɔn] clearance

precio especial

['presĭo espe'sĭal] special price

oferta especial

[o'fεrta espe'sĭal] special offer

Colors

Los colores [lɔs ko'lɔres]

el blanco
[ɛl 'blaŋko] white

el negro
[ɛl 'neɣro] black

el naranja
[ɛl na'raŋxa] orange

el marrón
[ɛl ma'rrɔn] brown

el gris
[ɛl gris] grey

el azul claro
[ɛl a'sul 'klaro]
light blue

claro	oscuro
[ˈklaro]	[osˈkuro]
light	dark

el rojo
[ɛl ˈrrɔxo] red

el rosa
[ɛl ˈrrɔsa] pink

el amarillo
[ɛl amaˈriʎo] yellow

el verde
[ɛl ˈbɛrðe] green

el azul oscuro
[ɛl aˈsul osˈkuro]
dark blue

el violeta
[ɛl bĭoˈleta] purple

Numbers

Los números [lɔs ˈnumeros]

0	cero	[ˈsero]
1	uno (un), una	[ˈuno (un) ˈuna]
2	dos	[dɔs]
3	tres	[tres]
4	cuatro	[ˈku̯atro]
5	cinco	[ˈsiŋko]
6	seis	[sɛi̯s]
7	siete	[ˈsi̯ete]
8	ocho	[ˈotʃo]
9	nueve	[ˈnu̯eβe]
10	diez	[di̯es]
11	once	[ˈɔnse]
12	doce	[ˈdose]
13	trece	[ˈtrese]
14	catorce	[kaˈtɔrse]
15	quince	[ˈkinse]
16	dieciséis	[di̯esiˈsɛi̯s]
17	diecisiete	[di̯esiˈsi̯ete]
18	dieciocho	[di̯esiˈotʃo]
19	diecinueve	[di̯esiˈnu̯eβe]
20	veinte	[ˈbɛi̯nte]
21	veintiuno	[bɛi̯nti̯ˈuno]
	(veintiún) veintiuna	[(bɛi̯nti̯ˈun) bɛi̯nti̯ˈuna]
22	veintidós	[bɛi̯ntiˈdɔs]
23	veintitrés	[bɛi̯ntiˈtres]
24	veinticuatro	[bɛi̯ntiˈku̯atro]

25	veinticinco	[bɛĭnti'siŋko]
26	veintiséis	[bɛĭnti'sɛĭs]
27	veintisiete	[bɛĭnti'sĭete]
28	veintiocho	[bɛĭnti'otʃo]
29	veintinueve	[bɛĭnti'nŭeβe]
30	treinta	['trɛĭnta]
40	cuarenta	[kŭa'renta]
50	cincuenta	[siŋ'kŭenta]
60	sesenta	[se'senta]
70	setenta	[se'tenta]
80	ochenta	[o'tʃenta]
90	noventa	[no'βenta]
100	cien	[sĭen]
101	ciento uno (un), una	['sĭento 'uno ('un) 'una]
200	doscientos(/as)	[dɔs'sĭentos/as]
300	trescientos(/as)	[tres'sĭentos/as]
400	cuatrocientos(/as)	[kŭatro'sĭentos/as]
500	quinientos(/as)	[ki'nĭentos/as]
600	seiscientos(/as)	[sɛĭs'sĭentos/as]
700	setecientos(/as)	[sete'sĭentos/as]
800	ochocientos(/as)	[otʃo'sĭentos/as]
900	novecientos(/as)	[noβe'sĭentos/as]
1000	mil	[mil]
1150	mil ciento cincuenta	[mil 'sĭento siŋ'kŭenta]
100 000	cien mil	[sĭen mil]
1 000 000	un millón	[un mi'ʎɔn]

1

el primero (primer) / la primera

[ɛl pri'mero (pri'mɛr) / la pri'mera]

the first

2

el segundo / la segunda

[ɛl se'ɣundo / la se'ɣunda]

the second

3

el tercero (tercer) / la tercera

[ɛl tɛr'sero (tɛr'sɛr) / la tɛr'sera]

the third

el cuarto / la cuarta [ɛl ˈkŭarto / la ˈkŭarta]	the fourth
el quinto / la quinta [ɛl ˈkinto / la ˈkinta]	the fifth
el sexto / la sexta [ɛl ˈsesto / la ˈsesta]	the sixth
el séptimo / la séptima [ɛl ˈsɛptimo / la ˈsɛptima]	the seventh
el octavo / la octava [ɛl ɔkˈtaβo / la ɔkˈtaβa]	the eighth
el noveno / la novena [ɛl noˈβeno / la noˈβena]	the ninth
el décimo / la décima [ɛl ˈdesimo / la ˈdesima]	the tenth

When then?

¿Cuándo entonces?
[ˈkŭando enˈtɔnses]

ayer
[aˈjɛr]
yesterday

---

anoche
[aˈnotʃe]]
yesterday evening

anteayer
[anteaˈjɛr]]
the day before yesterday

---

la semana pasada
[la seˈmana paˈsaða]]
last week

el año pasado
[ɛl ˈaɲo paˈsaðo]
last year

hoy
[ɔĭ]

today

mañana
[maˈɲana]

tomorrow

pasado mañana
[paˈsaðo maˈɲana]

the day after tomorrow

la semana que viene
[la seˈmana ke ˈbĭene]

next week

el año que viene
[ɛl ˈaɲo ke ˈbĭene]

next year

All about the time

Todo sobre la hora [ˈtoðo ˈsoβre la ˈora]

las horas [las ˈoras]	time
el reloj [ɛl rrɛˈlɔx]	clock
el segundo [ɛl seˈɣundo] los segundos [lɔs seˈɣundos]	second seconds
el minuto [ɛl miˈnuto] los minutos [lɔs miˈnutos]	minute minutes
un cuarto de hora [un ˈkŭarto de ˈora]	quarter of an hour
media hora [ˈmeðĭa ˈora]	half an hour
la hora [la ˈora] las horas [las ˈoras]	hour hours

la mañana

[la maˈɲana]

morning

el mediodía

[ɛl meðĭoˈðia]

noon

la tarde

[la ˈtarðe]

afternoon

la noche

[la ˈnotʃe]

night

la medianoche

[la meðĭaˈnotʃe]

midnight

early

[temˈprano]

early

late

[ˈtarðe]

late

¿Qué hora es?

[ke 'ora es]

What time is it?

Es la una.

[es la ˈuna]

It’s one a.m.

7:10

Son las siete y diez.

[sɔn las ˈsĭete i dĭes]

It’s ten past seven a.m.

7:15

Son las siete y cuarto.

[sɔn las ˈsĭete i ˈkŭarto]

It’s a quarter past seven a.m.

9:50

Son las diez menos diez.

[sɔn las dĭes ˈmenɔs dĭes]

It's ten to ten a.m.

10:00

Son las diez.

[sɔn las dĭes]

It's ten a.m.

10:10

Son las diez y diez.

[sɔn las dĭes i dĭes]

It's ten past ten a.m.

10:30

Son las diez y media.

[sɔn las dĭes i ˈmeðĭa]

It's half past ten a.m.

12:00

Son las doce del mediodía.

[sɔn las ˈdose del meðĭoˈdiːa]

It's midday.

19:55

Son las ocho menos cinco de la tarde

[sɔn las ˈotʃo ˈmenɔs ˈsiŋko de la ˈtarðe]

It's five to eight p.m.

20:00

Son las ocho de la tarde.

[sɔn las ˈotʃo de la ˈtarðe]

It's eight p.m.

24:00

Son las doce de la noche.

[sɔn las ˈdose de la ˈnotʃe]

It's midnight.

Seven days of the week

Los días de la semana

[lɔs 'diːas de la se'mana]

lunes	martes	miércoles
['lunes]	['martes]	['mĭɛrkoles]
Monday	Tuesday	Wednesday

el día laborable — work day

[ɛl 'diːa laβo'raβle]

el fin de semana — weekend

[ɛl fin de se'mana]

el día festivo — vacation

[ɛl 'dia fes'tiβo]

el día de descanso — rest day

[ɛl 'dia de des'kanso]

jueves ['xŭeβes]	**viernes** ['bĭɛrnes]	**sábado** ['saβaðo]	**domingo** [do'miŋgo]
Thursday	Friday	Saturday	Sunday

¿Qué día es hoy?
[ke 'dia es ɔĭ]

What day is it today?

Hoy es lunes.
[ɔĭ es 'lunes]

It's Monday.

¿Qué fecha es hoy?
[ke 'fetʃa es ɔĭ]

What date is it today?

Hoy es diez de enero.
[ɔĭ es dĭes de e'nero]

It's the 10th of January.

¿Hoy es festivo?
[ɔĭ es fes'tiβo]

Is today a holiday?

1

enero

[e'nero]
January

2

febrero

[fe'βrero]
February

5

mayo

['majo]
May

6

junio

['xunĭo]
June

9

septiembre

[sep'tĭembre]
September

10

octubre

[ɔk'tuβre]
October

The twelve months of the year

Los doce meses del año [lɔs ˈdose ˈmeses dɛl ˈaɲo]

3

marzo

[ˈmarso]
March

4

abril

[aˈβril]
April

7

julio

[ˈxulĭo]
July

8

agosto

[aˈɣɔsto]
August

11

noviembre

[noˈβĭembre]
November

12

diciembre

[diˈsĭembre]
December

The weather and seasons

El clima y las estaciones [ɛl ˈklima i las estaˈsĭɔnes]

la primavera [la primaˈβera] spring	el verano [ɛl beˈrano] summer
el otoño [ɛl oˈtoɲo] fall	el invierno [ɛl imˈbĭɛrno] winter

¿Qué tiempo hace hoy?	What's the weather like today?
[ke ˈtĭempo ˈasɛ ɔĭ]	
Hace buen tiempo.	The weather is fine today.
[ˈasɛ bŭen ˈtĭempo]	
Hace sol.	It's sunny.
[ˈasɛ sɔl]	
Hace mal tiempo.	The weather is bad today.
[ˈasɛ mal ˈtĭempo]	
Hace calor.	It's hot.
[ˈasɛ kaˈlɔr]	
Hace mucho calor.	It's very hot.
[ˈasɛ ˈmutʃo kaˈlɔr]	
Tengo mucho calor.	I'm boiling.
[ˈteŋgo ˈmutʃo kaˈlɔr]	
Hace mucho frío.	It's really cold.
[ˈasɛ ˈmutʃo ˈfrio]	
Tengo mucho frío.	I'm freezing.
[ˈteŋgo ˈmutʃo ˈfrio]	
Hace mucho viento.	It's windy.
[ˈasɛ ˈmutʃo ˈbĭento]	
Hay niebla.	It's foggy.
[aĭ ˈnĭeβla]	
Está lloviendo.	It's rainy.
[esˈta ʎoˈβĭendo]	
Está lloviznando.	It's drizzling.
[esˈta ʎoβisˈnando]	
Está nevando.	It's snowing.
[esˈta neˈβando]	

la frente
[la 'frente] forehead

el ojo
[ɛl 'ɔxo] eye

la nariz
[la na'ris] nose

la boca
[la 'boka] mouth

los dientes
[lɔs 'dĭentes] teeth

la lengua
[la 'leŋgŭa] tongue

la barbilla
[la bar'βiʎa] chin

los dedos
[lɔs 'deðos]
fingers

la mano
[la 'mano] hand

la cintura
[la sin'tura] waist

la cadera
[la ka'ðera] hip

Parts of the body

Las partes del cuerpo [las 'partes del 'kŭɛrpo]

la cabeza
[la ka'βesa] head
la cara
[la 'kara] face
las orejas
[las o'rɛxas] ear
la mejilla
[la mɛ'xiʎa] cheek
el cuello
[ɛl 'kŭeʎo] neck

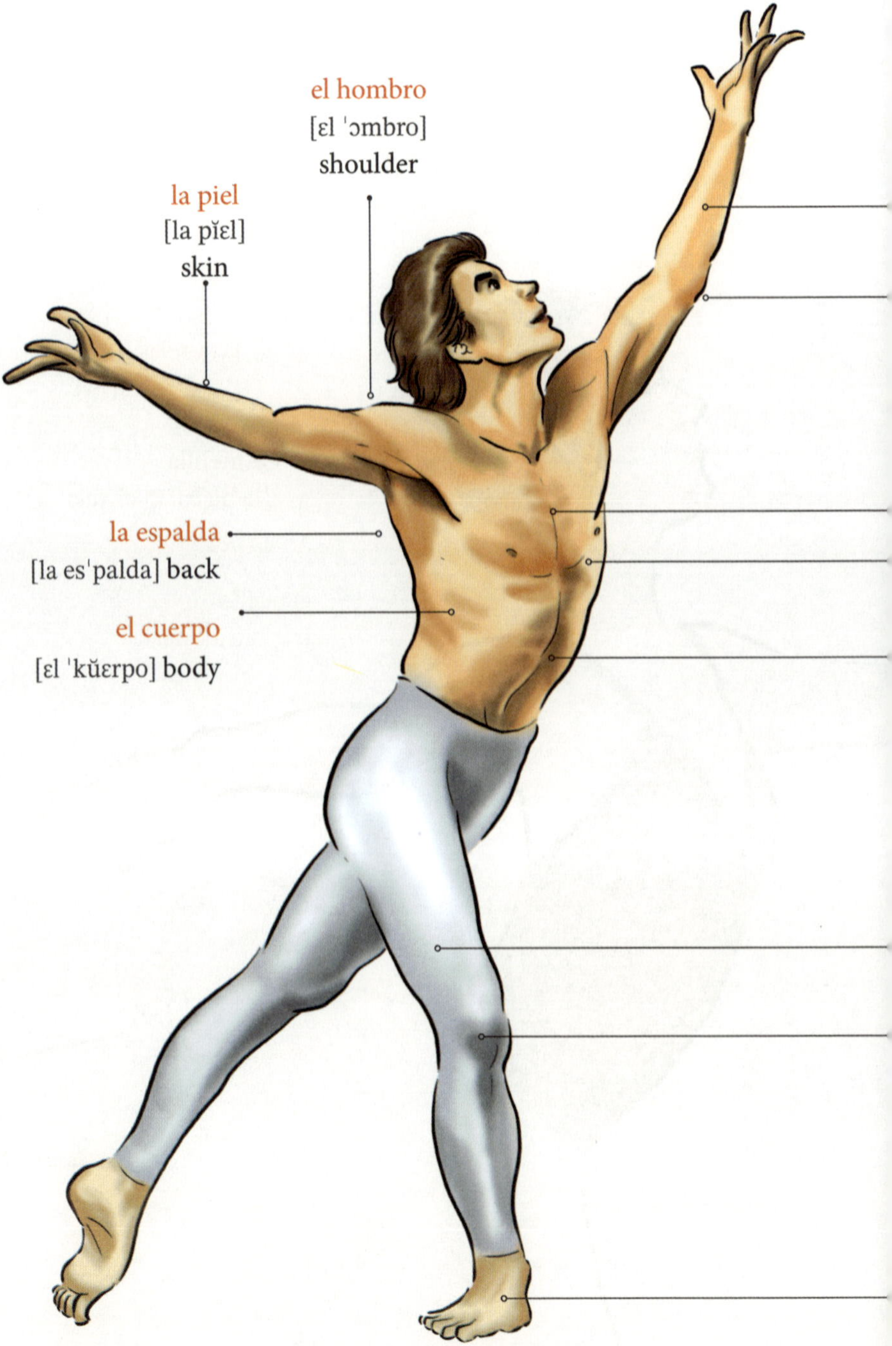
el hombro
[ɛl ˈɔmbro]
shoulder
la piel
[la pĭɛl]
skin
la espalda
[la esˈpalda] back
el cuerpo
[ɛl ˈkŭɛrpo] body

el brazo
[ɛl ˈbraso] arm

el codo
[ɛl ˈkoðo] elbow

el pecho
[ɛl ˈpetʃo] chest

el corazón
[ɛl koraˈsɔn] heart

la barriga
[la baˈrriɣa] stomach

la pierna
[la ˈpĭɛrna] leg

la rodilla
[la rrɔˈðiʎa] knee

el pie
[ɛl pĭe] foot

When you feel sick

Cuando se siente mal ['kŭando se 'sĭente mal]

Estoy enfermo/a. [es'tɔĭ em'fɛrmo/a]	I don't feel well.
Tengo que vomitar. ['teŋgo ke bomi'tar]	I need to vomit.
Tengo náuseas. ['teŋgo 'naŭseas]	I feel nauseous.
Me duele aquí. [me 'dŭele a'ki]	It hurts here.
Tengo fiebre. ['teŋgo 'fĭeβre]	I have a fever.
Me duele la cabeza. [me 'dŭele la ka'βesa]	I have a headache.
Me duele la barriga. [me 'dŭele la ba'rriɣa]	I have a stomachache.

Me duele la garganta. [me ˈdŭele la garˈɣanta]	I have a sore throat.
Me duele la espalda. [me ˈdŭele la esˈpalda]	I have backache.
Tengo dolor de muelas. [ˈteŋgo doˈlɔr de ˈmŭelas]	I have a toothache.
Tengo estreñimiento. [ˈteŋgo estreɲiˈmĭento]	I am constipated.
Tengo diarrea. [ˈteŋgo dĭaˈrrɛa]	I have diarrhoea.
Tengo alergia. [ˈteŋgo aˈlɛrxia]	I have an allergy.
Tengo un sarpullido. [ˈteŋgo un sarpuˈʎiðo]	I have a rash.

la farmacia

[la farˈmasi̯a] pharmacy

el hospital

[ɛl ɔspiˈtal] hospital

el médico

[ɛl ˈmeðiko] doctor

la médica

[la ˈmeðika] doctor

el enfermero

[ɛl emfɛrˈmero] (male) nurse

la enfermera

[la emfɛrˈmera] (female) nurse

la medicina / el medicamento

[la meðiˈsina / ɛl meðikaˈmento] medicine

¡Jesús! / ¡Salud!

[xeˈsus / saˈluð]

Bless you!

Everyday activities

Las Actividades diarias [las aktiβiˈðaðes ðiˈarĭas]

despertarse
[desperˈtarse]
wake up

levantarse
[leβanˈtarse]
get up

cepillarse los dientes
[sepiˈʎarse lɔs ˈdĭentes]
brush teeth

ducharse
[duˈtʃarse]
take a shower

tomar un baño
[toˈmar um ˈbaɲo]
take a bath

cocinar
[kosi'nar]
cook

comer
[ko'mer]
eat

beber
[be'βer]
drink

leer
[le'er]
read

escribir
[eskri'βir]
write

mirar
[mi'rar]
look at

esperar
[espe'rar]
wait

encontrarse
[eŋkon'trarse]
meet

dar
[dar]
give

satisfacer
[satisfa'ser]
be glad

bailar
[bai'lar]
dance

reír
[re'ir]
laugh

llorar
[ʎo'rar]
cry

abandonar
[aβando'nar]
leave

llamar por teléfono
[ʎa'mar por te'lefono]
call on the telephone

hacer deporte
[a'sɛr de'pɔrte]
do sports

pintar
[pin'tar]
paint

observar
[oβser'βar]
watch

cantar
[kan'tar]
sing

fotografiar / tomar fotografías
[fotoɣra'fjar / to'mar fotoɣra'fias]
take pictures

divertirse
[diβer'tirse]
have fun

comprar
[kom'prar]
buy

vender
[ben'dɛr]
sell

trabajar
[traβa'xar]
work

enseñar
[enseˈɲar]
teach

aprender
[aprenˈder]
learn

abrazar
[aβraˈsar]
hug

amar
[aˈmar]
love

besar
[beˈsar]
kiss

casarse
[kaˈsarse]
marry

Urgency

Urgencias [ur'xensĭas]

¿Dónde está el lavabo?

['dɔnde es'ta ɛl la'βaβo]

Where is the toilet?

Necesito ir al lavabo.

[nese'sito ir al la'βaβo]

I need to go to the toilet.

¿Hay un baño público por aquí?

[aĭ un ˈbaɲo ˈpuβliko pɔr aˈki]

Is there a public toilet near here?

¡Necesito ir al hospital en seguida!

[neseˈsito ir al ɔspiˈtal en seˈɣiða]

I need to go to the hospital.

¡Llame a la policía, por favor!

[ˈʎame a la poliˈsia pɔr faˈβɔr]

Call the police, please!

¡Cuidado!

[kŭiˈðaðo] Watch out!

¡Socorro!

[soˈkɔrro] Help!

¡Fuego!

['fŭeɣo] Fire!

¡Emergencia!

[emɛr'xensĭa] Emergency

What do these signs mean?

¿Qué nos dicen las señales? [ke nɔs 'disen las se' ɲales]

¡PELIGRO!
[pe'liɣro]

DANGER

NO ENTRAR
[no en'trar]

NO ENTRY

¡ALTO! NO PASAR
['alto no pa'sar]

RESTRICTED AREA

PELIGRO ELECTRICIDAD
[pe'liɣro elɛktrisi'ðað]

ELECTRICAL HAZARD

SENTIDO ÚNICO
[senˈtiðo ˈuniko]

ONE WAY

NO ESTACIONAR
[no estasĭoˈnar]

NO PARKING

ENTRADA Y SALIDA DE VEHÍCULOS
[enˈtraða y saˈliða de beˈikulos]

PLEASE DO NOT PARK
VEHICLES EXIT

DESVÍO
[dezˈβio]

DIVERSION

ÁREA DE ESTACIONAMIENTO
[ˈarea de estasĭonaˈmĭento]

PARKING AREA

PRIMEROS AUXILIOS
[pri'meros aŭɣ'silĭos]

FIRST AID

EMERGENCIAS
[emɛr'xensĭas]

EMERGENCY

ZONA ESCOLAR
[sona esko'lar]

SCHOOL ZONE

¡ATENCIÓN! CUIDADO CON EL PERRO
[aten'sĭɔn kŭi'ðaðo kɔn el 'pɛrro]

CAUTION! BITING DOG

PLAN DE EVACUACIÓN

[plan de eβakŭaˈsĭon]

EVACUATION PLAN

SALIDA DE EMERGENCIA

[saˈliða de emɛrˈxensĭa]

EMERGENCY EXIT

SOLO PERSONAL AUTORIZADO

[ˈsolo pɛrsoˈnal aŭtoriˈsaðo]

AUTHORIZED PERSONNEL ONLY

ZONA PEATONAL

[ˈsona peatoˈnal]

PEATONAL ZONE

CORREOS

CORREOS
[kɔ'rrɛos]

POST

CINE
['sine]

CINEMA

NO MOLESTAR
[no moles'tar]

DO NOT DISTURB

NO FUMAR
[no fu'mar]

NO SMOKING

DAMAS
['damas]

WOMEN

CABALLEROS
[kaβa'ʎeros]

MEN

ABIERTO
[aˈβĭɛrto]

OPEN

CERRADO
[sɛˈrraðo]

CLOSED

AUTOSERViCIO
[aŭtɔsɛrˈβisĭo]

SELF-SERVICE

RESERVADO
[rrɛsɛrˈβaðo]

RESERVED

NO INGERIR ALIMENTOS
EN ESTA AREA
[no iŋxeˈrir aliˈmentos en ˈesta ˈarea]

DO NOT EAT FOOD
IN THIS AREA

Emotional outbursts

In this chapter we will be dealing with something rather special: emotional outbursts. What, you may ask, does this have to do with a book aimed at introducing a foreign language?

I know that this is quite a sensitive issue and I'm pretty sure that you don't know any other language books that deal with the topic. As I say, I'm inviting you on a risky adventure. But I think it's absolutely essential for you and really useful. I think you need to know this because it can help you to avoid very embarrassing situations when you are in Mexico.

First, let me explain what I mean by emotional outbursts. What exactly are they? They are words that simply tumble out of your mouth. You don't usually give them a second thought – they just pop out – and can't be popped back in again, once they're out.

When we are angry, disappointed, afraid, surprised or delighted, we use emotional outbursts to let off steam and regain our calm. We can think of them as turbulence tranquilizers for our emotions.

These outbursts can be more or less violent, depending on intonation and the particular intention or situation in which they are spoken. Gentle outbursts can be mumbled to ourselves to cool our spirits. Violent emotional outbursts are often insulting and deeply hurtful. This type is known in Spanish as "palabrotas" or "groserías" .

So, you can probably now appreciate how difficult and tricky this whole topic is. These words and phrases are used unconsciously all the time all over the world. The fact that I bring up this topic may be unpleasant for the Mexican who are often reserved and polite by nature. However, my intentions are entirely good. I don't want to insult or ridicule their language, but simply to help you avoid making a fool of yourself.

If you hear these Spanish words and try to copy them, it's more than likely that you'll get the exact intonation wrong, or it won't come out at quite the right moment, or be appropriate for the person or situation you're in.

So, my first tip is: don't block your ears when you hear them, but don't just copy them either. As a foreigner, you need to get to know them but use them carefully, and only if you're absolutely certain about how and when.

But even if you never use these outbursts yourself, it is certainly helpful to know them. It might avoid a few embarrassing situations or even a slap around the face. This is one of the main reasons for dealing with these phrases.

I hope I've been able to make clear why this topic is an important one in language learning.

Let's get started:

The first word we will be dealing with is the word "¡Mierda!". This word literally means the organic waste matter from the digestive system. There is a corresponding word in English but it would be bad manners to print it here. Everyone knows the word, and similar word exists in every language so I do not need to add anything.

You will also hear the word "Estúpido" which is a translation of "stupid". I don't think I need to add much by way of explanation. Referring to the limits of someone's intellegence is a common way of insulting someone all over the world. Perhaps I should add that if the person in question is female, the Mexicans will use the feminine form: "Estúpida".

A slightly stronger version of the same idea is the word "Idiota". We all know what being called an idiot means, so I don't need to add much. In this case Mexicans will use the same word whether they are referring to a man or a woman.

Now let's turn to stronger expressions. Most decent Mexicans might be horrified to read the following words, and could consider a reference to them as an insult to their language. As I have already said, this is not my intention in writing this book.

In order to respect their feelings, I have decided to use a kind of code. I will not write the word itself but use a Spanish phonetic alphabet table. This also has the useful side effect that you will learn how to spell the words.

The first two emotinal outbursts in this category can be coded as follows:

Pedro, Elephante, Nena, Dedo, Elephante, Julio, Óscar.
and
Coche, Uva, Limón, Elephante, Roberto, Óscar.

These two words are rather harsh. Either expression will give you the opportunity to speak your mind or communicate your opinions, the same way as "You idiot!" or "Asshole!" in English does.

The next set of outburst is very common and is used on a daily basis in Mexico. Let's face it, it is something that is common to all languages. The outburst in question is:

Vaca, Elephante, Roberto, García, Ana.

Literally it is a vulgar reference to the male genitalia. Here are the extended forms of use:

"¡Vales **v....**!" = You're worth a male genitalia!
"¡Vete a la **v....**!" = Go to hell!

The following expression is an outburst made up of three words. It's a swear word that describes the son of a lady, whose profession involves a lot of lying down. In fact, the speaker is not referring to a particular profession nor is he interested in any family relationships. What the term really expresses is an extremely rude way of insulting someone. Here are the words in coded form:

Hola, Ignacio, Julio, Óscar
Dedo, Elephante
Pedro, Uva, Tenedor, Ana

The red-light district also provides a further emotional outburst that is quite common in Spanish. Her is the word in code form:

Pedro, Uva, Tenedor, Ana Mama, Ana, Dedo, Roberto, Elephante

The word-for-word translation is "prostitute mother". However, as in previous examples, this is not what is really meant. In fact when this expression is use, it may not even relate to a woman at all. It is rather an expression of extreme surprise or chock.

Finally, dear readers, let me assure you that I have tried to do all I can to deal with such a sensitive and controversial issue without embarrassing you. I strongly believe that it is important to give you as much confidence as possible when starting to learn the Spanish language.

Knowing something about how people express their feelings and emotions is part of that process. I could continue on this theme for some time, but it's enough for you to have a clear idea of the topic, so that you can avoid any embarrassing situations.

Never forget that emotional outburst can vary in meaning as well as in intensity. If you hear one of these phrases, see if you can hear whether the speaker is angry, dissatisfied, furious, or perhaps cracking a joke or making fun of someone.

As far as possible, avoid using these outbursts yourself. Remember, that these words have the power to insult and hurt others and can also be dangerous for you. By using them you are likely to put yourself in a very embarrassing situation, and quite possibly lose face in the process.

¡Bravo!
['braβo] **Bravo!**

¡Genial!
[xe'nĭal] **Awesome!**

¡Estupendo!
[estu'pendo] **Great!**

¡Excelente!
[esse'lente] **Excellent!**

Compliments

Cumplidos [kumˈpliðos]

¡Espléndido!
[esˈplendiðo]

Splendid!

¡Maravilloso!
[maraβiˈʎoso]

Marvelous!

Romance

Romántico [rrɔˈmantiko]

Eres muy guapo/a.

[ˈeres mŭi gŭapo/a]

You are so handsome / beautiful.

Tienes unos ojos bonitos.

[ˈtĭenes ˈunos ˈɔxos boˈnitos]

You have got beautiful eyes.

Eres extraordinario/a.

[ˈeres estraɔrðiˈnarĭo/a]

You are extraordinary.

Me gustas mucho.

[me ˈgustas ˈmutʃo]

I like you very much.

Te quiero mucho.

[te ˈkĭero ˈmutʃo]

I love you very much.

Eres tan hermoso/a.

[ˈeres tan ɛrˈmoso/a]

You are so beautiful.

Eres único/a.

['eres'uniko/a]

You are special.

Te amo.

[te 'amo]

I love you.

Te amo con locura.

[te ˈamo kɔn loˈkura]

I love you so much.

¿Quieres casarte conmigo?

[ˈki̯eres kaˈsarte kɔnˈmiɣo]

Will you marry me?

Land and people

El país y su gente [ɛl paˈis i su ˈxente]

If you want to learn about the shape and form of Mexico, the simplest thing to do is to look at a map. If you want to know more about the people, how they think, how they lead their lives, then the best method is to look at their proverbs. They reveal how the Mexicans "tick".

Often proverbs have developed over centuries as the result of local people's experiences and of the way they think and live their lives. These sayings are passed on from one generation to the next, together with the emotions and moods they convey. Here are a few memorable Mexican proverbs:

> Mejor solo que mal acompañado.
> [meˈxoɾ ˈsolo ke mal akompaˈɲado]
> Better alone than In bad company.
>
> El que se enoja, pierde.
> [el ke se eˈno.xa ˈpĭɛrðe]
> The one who gets mad loses.
>
> A quien madruga, Dios lo ayuda.
> [a ˈkĭen maˈdruɣa ˈdios lo aˈjuða]
> God helps the one who wakes up early.
>
> Poco a poco se anda lejos
> [ˈpoko a ˈpoko se ˈanda lexos]
> Little by little one goes far.
>
> Agua que no has de beber, déjala correr.
> [ˈaɣŭa ke no as de beˈβɛr ˈdexala kɔˈrrɛr]
> Water you don't have to drink, let it run.

Now you will be able to savor the Spanish language like a delicatessen. Any worries you may have had about learning this language will turn to joyful confidence.

Spanish
at your Fingertips

by
Tien Tammada

Original title: สเปนทันใจพูดได้ด้วยปลายนิ้ว เฑียร ธรรมดา

232 Moo 3, Tambon Yangneung, Sarapee District,
Chiangmai 50140 Thailand
E-Mail: leelaaphasa2008@gmail.com

1. Edition 2025 (1,01 - 2025)

Translation: Ta Tammadien, Hubert Möller, David Thron
Proofreader: Alejandro Garrido, Kidan Patanant, Vicente García, Almudena García Hernández, Klangjai Patanant
Cover Design: Leonie Eul, Aimée Lorenz
Illustration Inside: K. Kiattisak, Purmpoon Khamnuanta
Photo Credit Cover: Mexican Flag: Milano M/Shutterstock; Chichén Itzá: Art of Ngu/Adobe Stock; Food Cart: primiaou/Adobe Stock; Sugar Skull: Sukho/Adobe Stock
Typesetting/Layout: Wachana Leuwattananon, Mienton Pantana
Printing: Multiprint Ltd., Konstinbrod

ISBN 978-3-12-614006-5